First Facts®

Primary Source Pro



Research

# Visual Primary Sources

## Photographs, Paintings, Video, and More!

by Kelly Boswell

PEBBLE
a capstone imprint

First Facts are published by Pebble
1710 Roe Crest Drive, North Mankato, Minnesota 56003
www.mycapstone.com



**Library of Congress Cataloging-in-Publication Data**
Library of Congress Cataloging-in-Publication-Data is on file with the Library of Congress.
ISBN 978-1-9771-0289-8 (library binding)
ISBN 978-1-9771-0513-4 (paperback)
ISBN 978-1-9771-0293-5 (ebook pdf)

**Editorial Credits**
Erika L. Shores, editor; Charmaine Whitman, designer; Jo Miller, media researcher; Laura Manthe, production specialist

**Image Credits**
Alamy: Classicstock, Cover (top right), Pictorial Press Ltd, 17; Dreamstime: Spotmatik, 5; Library of Congress Prints and Photographs/Baseball Cards from the Benjamin K. Edwards Collection, Cover (bottom left); NASA, 13; Shutterstock: Everett Historical, Cover (top left), Hank Frentz, 6 (bottom right), pook_jun, 6 (bottom left), tongcom photographer, 19, vilax, Cover (bottom right) 6 (top right); Wikimedia: NARA, 21, NASA, 11, The Metropolitan Museum of Art/Emanuel Leutze, 9, United States Information Agency, 15, Wrigley's, 7

**Design Elements**
Shutterstock: azure1, iABC

Printed and bound in the United States of America.
1869

# Table of Contents

# Introduction

Have you ever looked through a family photo album? The picture of your grandfather as a boy might surprise you!

Photographs are **primary sources**. Primary sources are recorded, written, or created by people who lived at the time. They help us learn more about people, places, and events from the past.

**primary source**—an original, first-hand account of an event or time period

smile LOVE
FRIENDS laugh
happy Family
friends good times
Love
Believe
hope

# Different Kinds of Visual Primary Sources

Photographs, video clips, paintings, and advertisements (ads) are different kinds of **visual** primary sources.

World War I took place from 1914 until 1918. That means that Wrigley's gum was around even earlier than 1914.

**Fact**

Ads like this one help us know more about life in the past. Back then, a pack of gum cost only 5 cents!

**visual**—something you look at, such as a picture, chart, or video, that is used to make something more appealing or easier to understand

Paintings are a visual primary source. When you **examine** a painting, first notice what is happening in the painting. Then, notice and name all of the objects you see. Look carefully!

**Fact**

In 1851 Emanuel Leutze painted George Washington and his army crossing the Delaware River on Christmas night in 1776. The army was hoping to attack the British troops in Trenton, New Jersey.

**examine**—to inspect or look at something carefully

There are several boats loaded with men and horses.

There are boats, ropes, paddles, swords, and a flag. There are large chunks of ice in the river.

Photographs record a moment in time. In this photograph from 1966, we see astronauts waiting to be lifted out of the water. They had returned from 14 days in space.

Astronauts Neil Armstrong and David Scott (sitting in capsule) were members of the *Gemini VIII* spaceflight.

# Looking Closely, Learning More

When looking at visual sources, imagine wearing a special pair of glasses that help you to be a careful **observer**. Look closely at the *entire* visual. Start at the top and go all the way to the bottom. What are you thinking when you first look at it? What are you wondering?

**Fact**

The D-558-1 *Skystreak* was designed to find out more about flying at fast speeds. It set a world speed record in 1947, traveling at speeds of 650 miles (1,046 kilometers) per hour!

**observer**—a person who becomes aware of things by looking at them closely

NASA Dryden Flight Research Center Photo Collection
http://www.dfrc.nasa.gov/gallery/photo/index.html
NASA Photo: E49-059 Date: 1949

D-558-1 on ramp with ground crew

Captions tell us when the photo was taken and what is in the photo.

Another way to examine and record your thinking about visual primary sources is to answer the "Five W Questions."

| | |
|---|---|
| **Who?** | Are there people in the visual? Who are they? |
| **What?** | What is going on in the visual? What story is this visual trying to tell? |
| **Where?** | Where do you think the event happened? |
| **When?** | When was the visual created? |
| **Why?** | Why do you think this visual was created? |

**segregation**—separating people because of their skin color

**civil rights movement**—in the 1950s and 1960s, an effort to gain African Americans equal treatment in the United States

**What:** The people are carrying signs that talk about voting rights, **segregation**, and jobs.

**Who:** Martin Luther King Jr. is in the photo. He is surrounded by lots of other people, men and women, black and white.

**Why:** The photographer wanted to record an important moment in time.

**Where:** The photo was taken outside. From the photo, we can't tell for sure in what city it was taken.

**When:** Since there are no dates on the photograph, we can't know for sure when the photo was taken. But we know that King was a leader in the **civil rights movement** from 1955 until he died in 1968.

Your turn! Use the "Five W Questions" to study this ad from 1865.

| | |
|---|---|
| **Who?** | Who are the people in the visual? |
| **What?** | What is going on in the visual? What story is this visual trying to tell? |
| **Where?** | Where do you think the event happened? |
| **When?** | When was the visual created? |
| **Why?** | Why do you think this visual was created? |

This ad shows women using a machine to wash clothing.

WASHING MACHINE & WRINGER.
HOME
WASHER

# Looking Beyond Visuals

Think about putting together a puzzle. There are many pieces that fit together to make the whole picture.

We can learn a lot from visual sources. But they only give us one piece of the whole puzzle. We need to look at books, websites, and other sources. They help us see the whole picture.

A picture of Chief Joseph can give us some information about him and the Nez Percé Indian Tribe. But it is only one piece of the puzzle. Other visuals, documents, speeches, and objects from the Nez Percé can help us see the whole picture. We can find out who Chief Joseph was and what he did.

**Fact**

Chief Joseph was the leader of the Nez Percé. In 1877 he gave up his homeland to the U.S. government in a famous speech.

*"My people, some of them, have run away to the hills and have no blankets, no food. No one knows where they are—perhaps freezing to death. I want to have time to look for my children and see how many I can find. Maybe I shall find them among the dead. Hear me, my chiefs. I am tired. My heart is sick and sad. From where the sun now stands, I will fight no more forever."*

*—Chief Joseph, 1877*

## Glossary

**civil rights movement**—in the 1950s and 1960s, an effort to gain African Americans equal treatment in the United States

**examine**—to inspect or look at something carefully

**observer**—a person who becomes aware of things by looking at them closely

**primary source**—an original, first-hand account of an event or time period

**segregation**—separating people because of their skin color

**visual**—something you look at, such as a picture, chart, or video, that is used to make something more appealing or easier to understand

## Read More

**Barghoorn, Linda.** *Be a Photograph Detective.* Be a Document Detective. New York: Crabtree Publishing Company, 2017.

**Clapper, Nikki Bruno.** *Learning About Primary Sources.* Media Literacy for Kids. North Mankato, Minn.: Capstone Press, 2016.

## Internet Sites

Use FactHound to find Internet sites related to this book.

Visit *www.facthound.com*

Just type in 9781977102898 and go.

## Critical Thinking Questions

1. Can you find an old photograph of someone in your family? What can you learn about that person by looking carefully at the photograph?
2. What kinds of visual sources are we leaving behind for people in the future? What do you think these visuals will tell them about us?
3. Why is it important to take your time and look closely at a visual? Use the text to help you.

## Index